Rhythm Of Love

Reduce Stress Coloring book

By

S.B. Nozaz

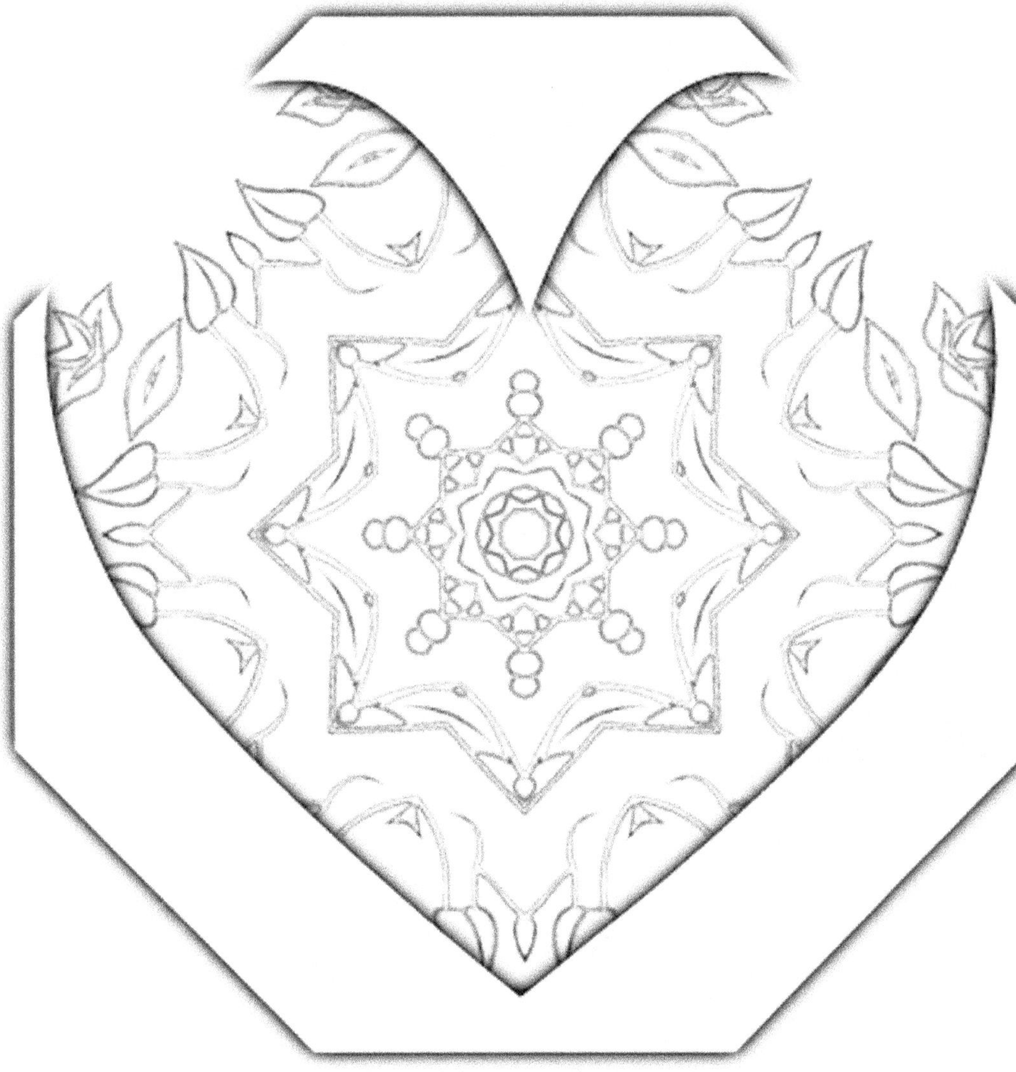

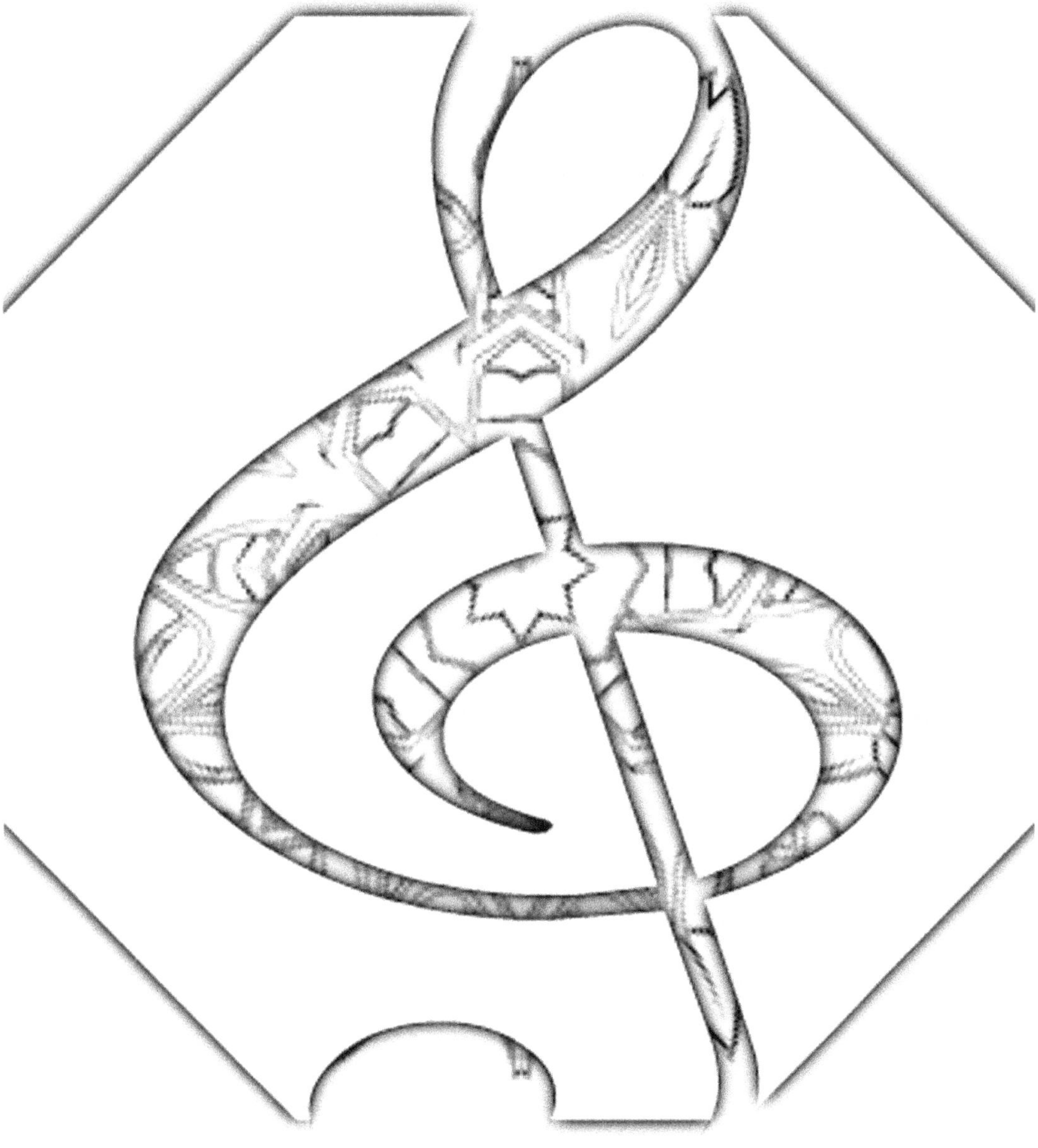

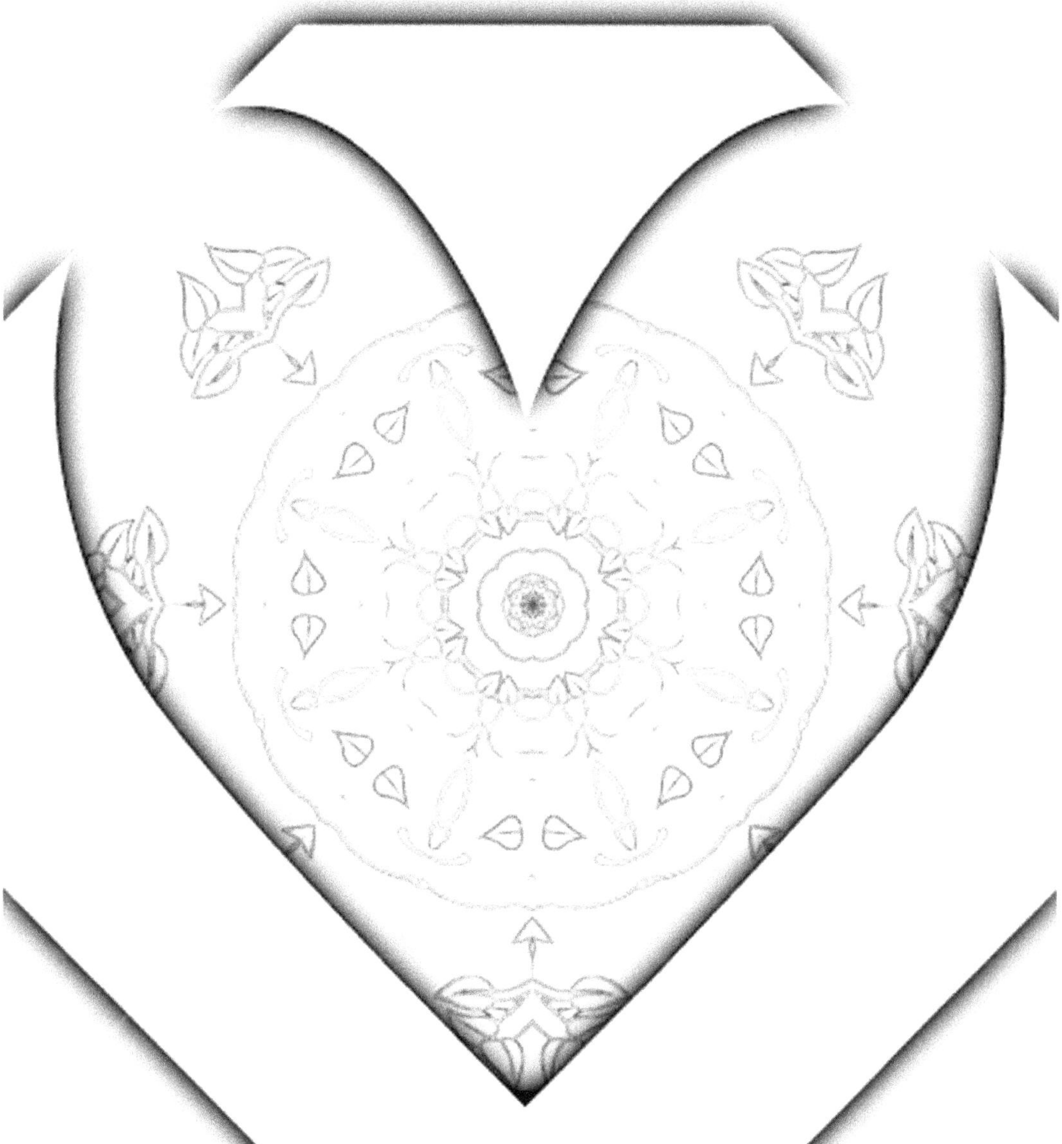

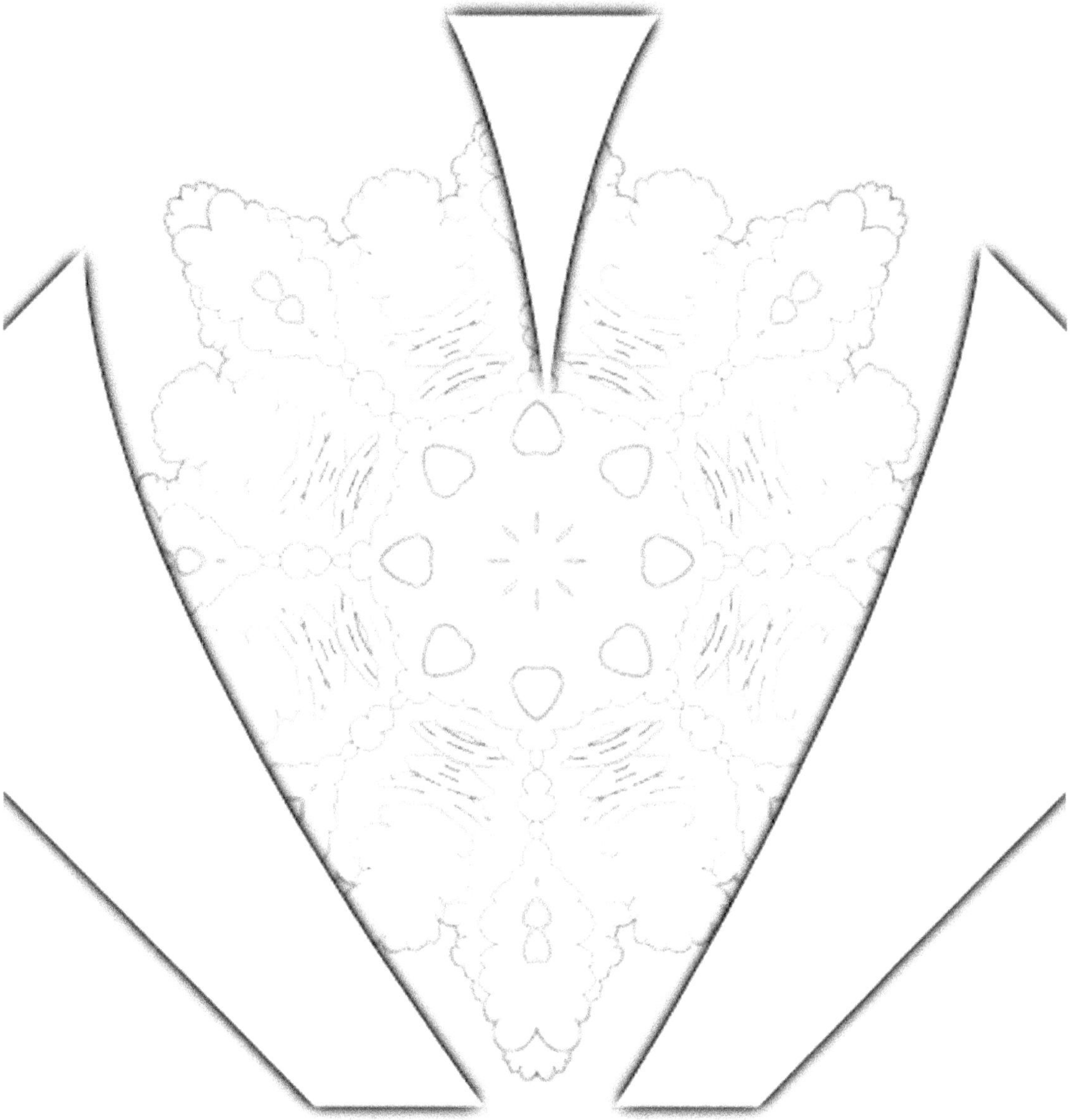

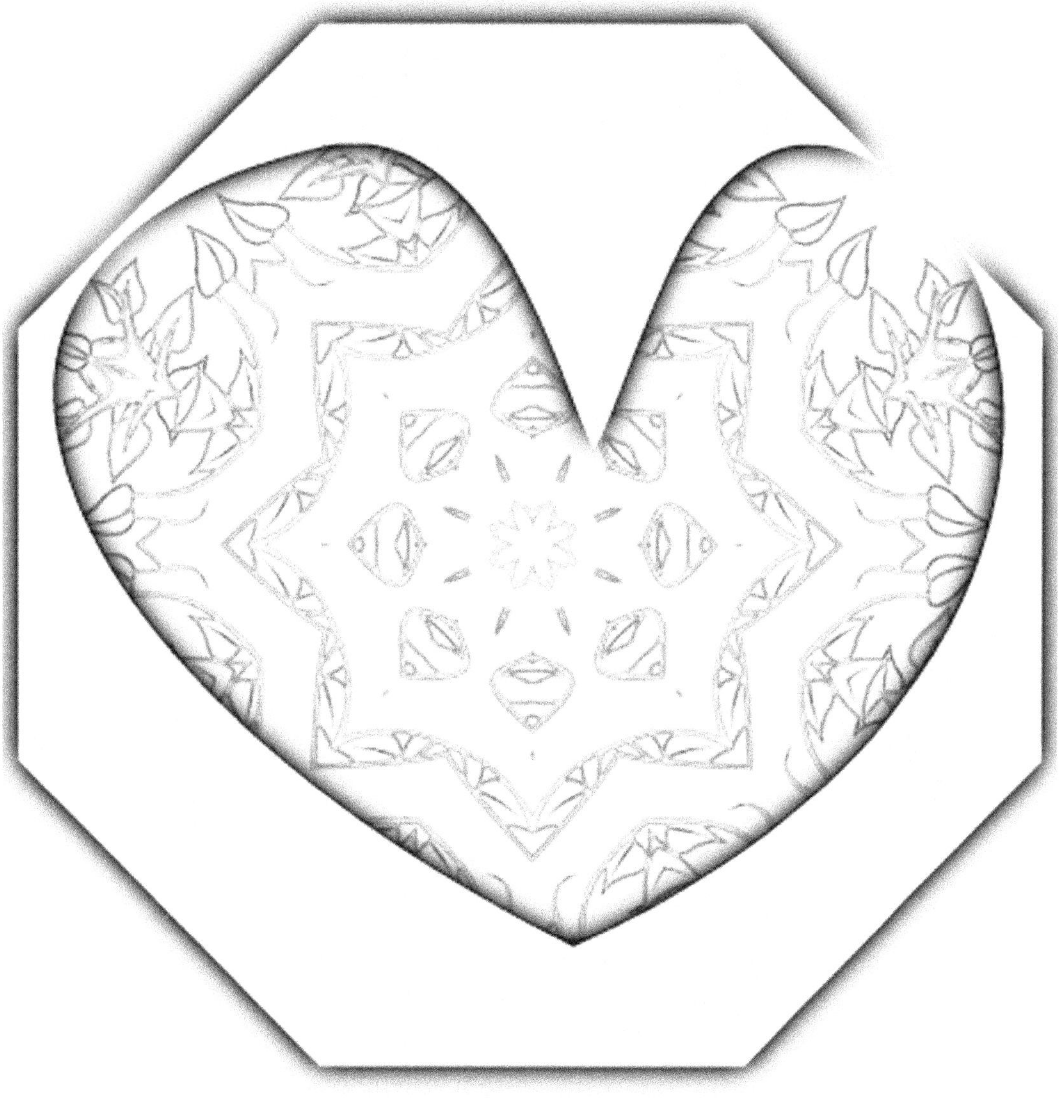

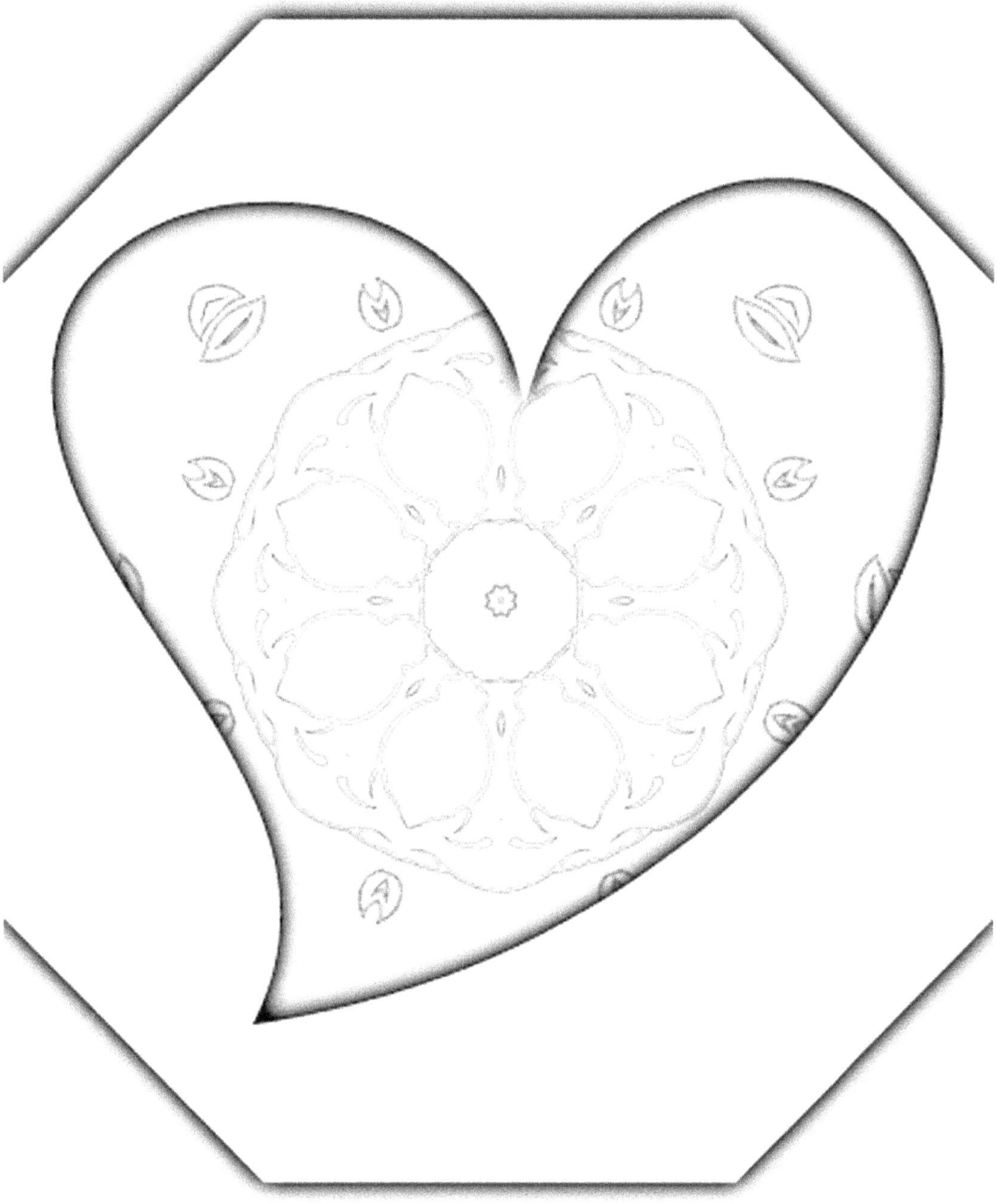

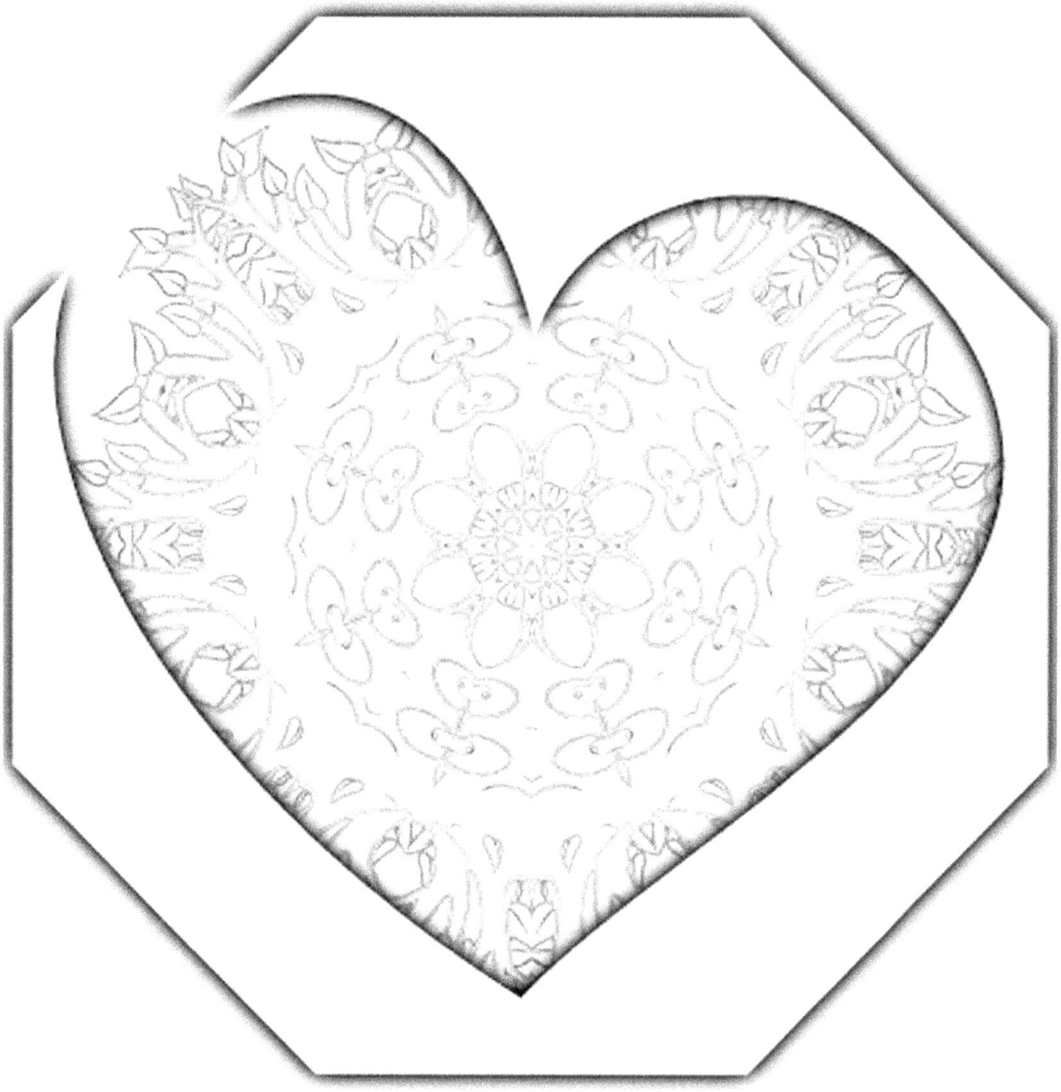

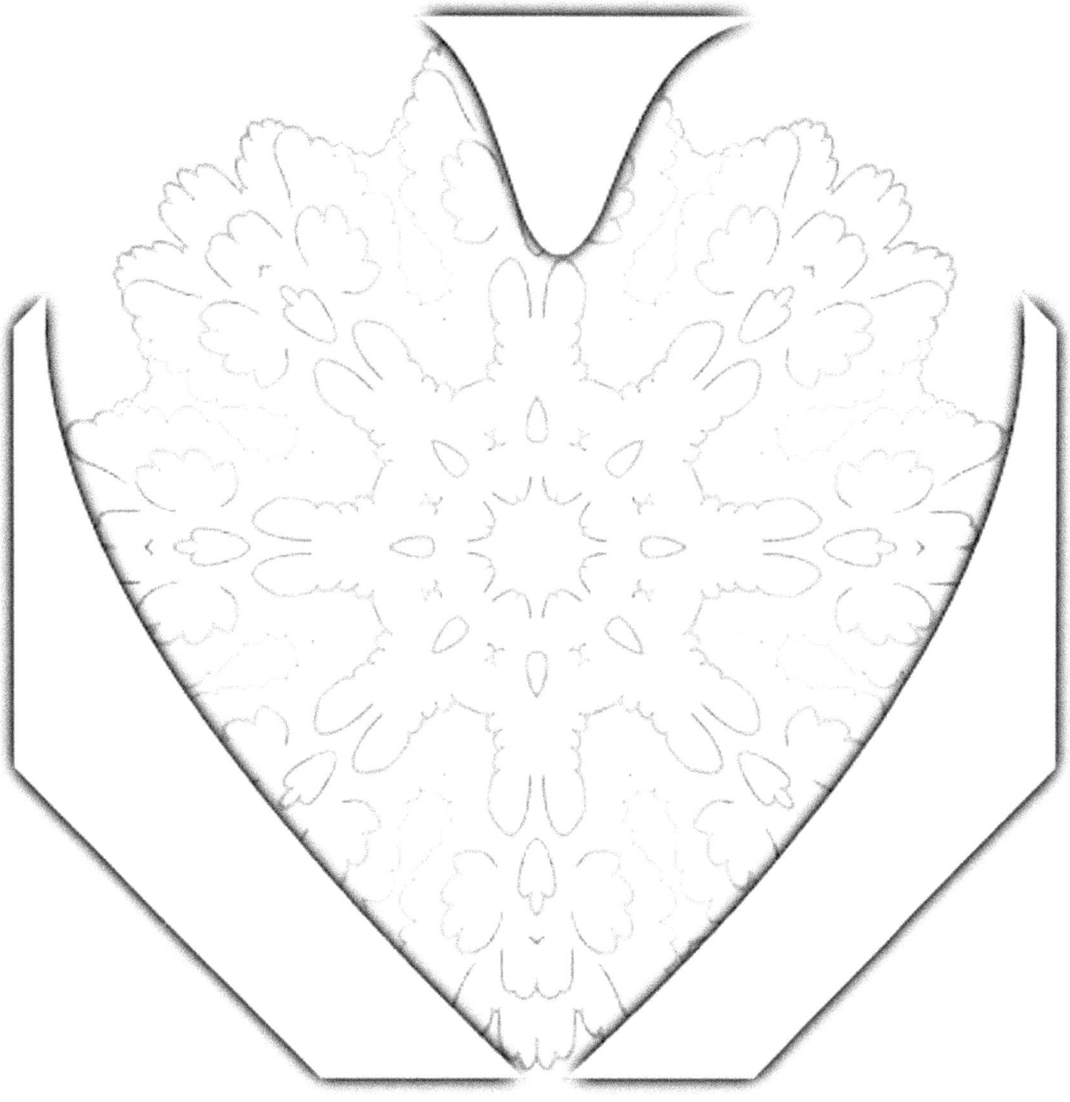

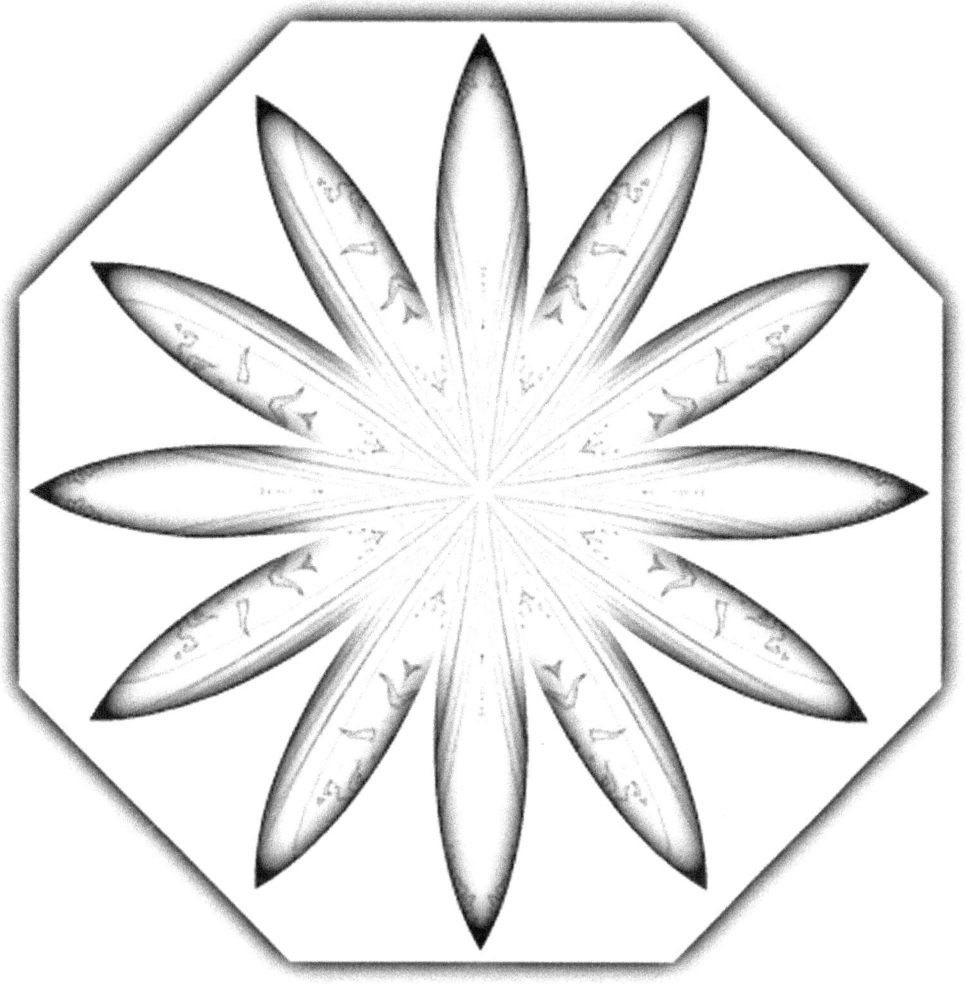

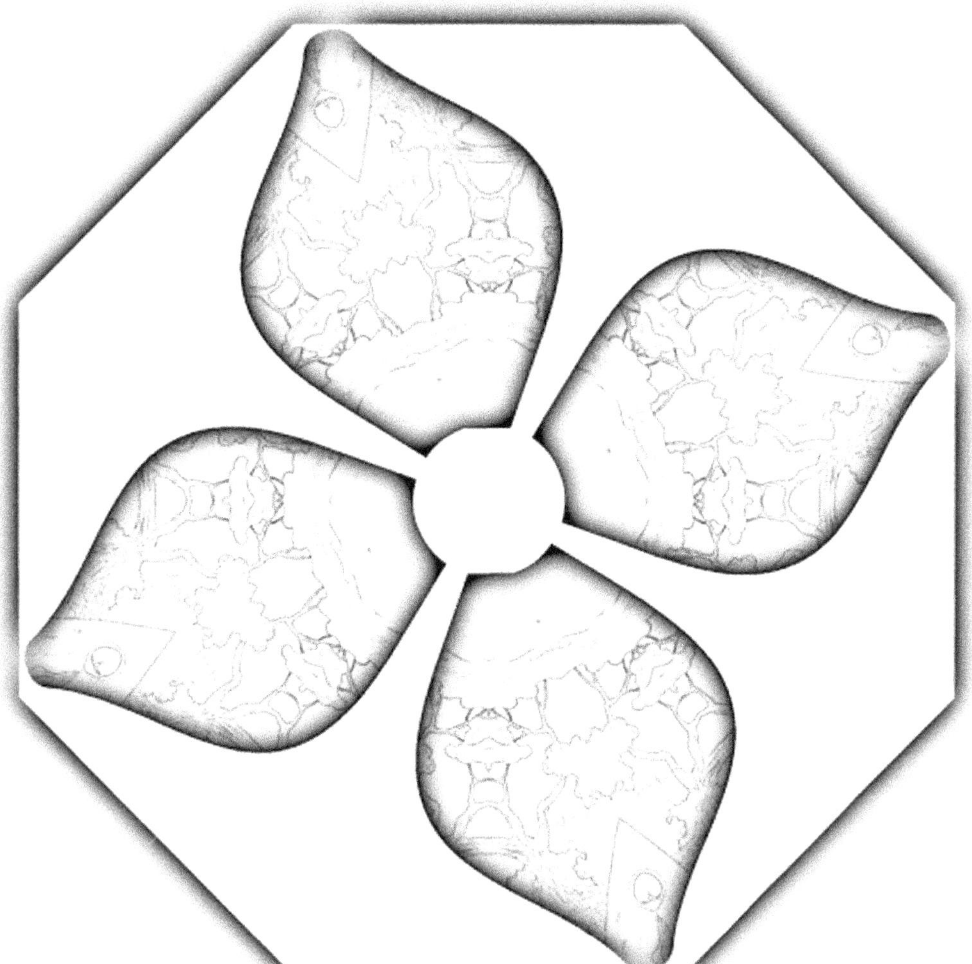

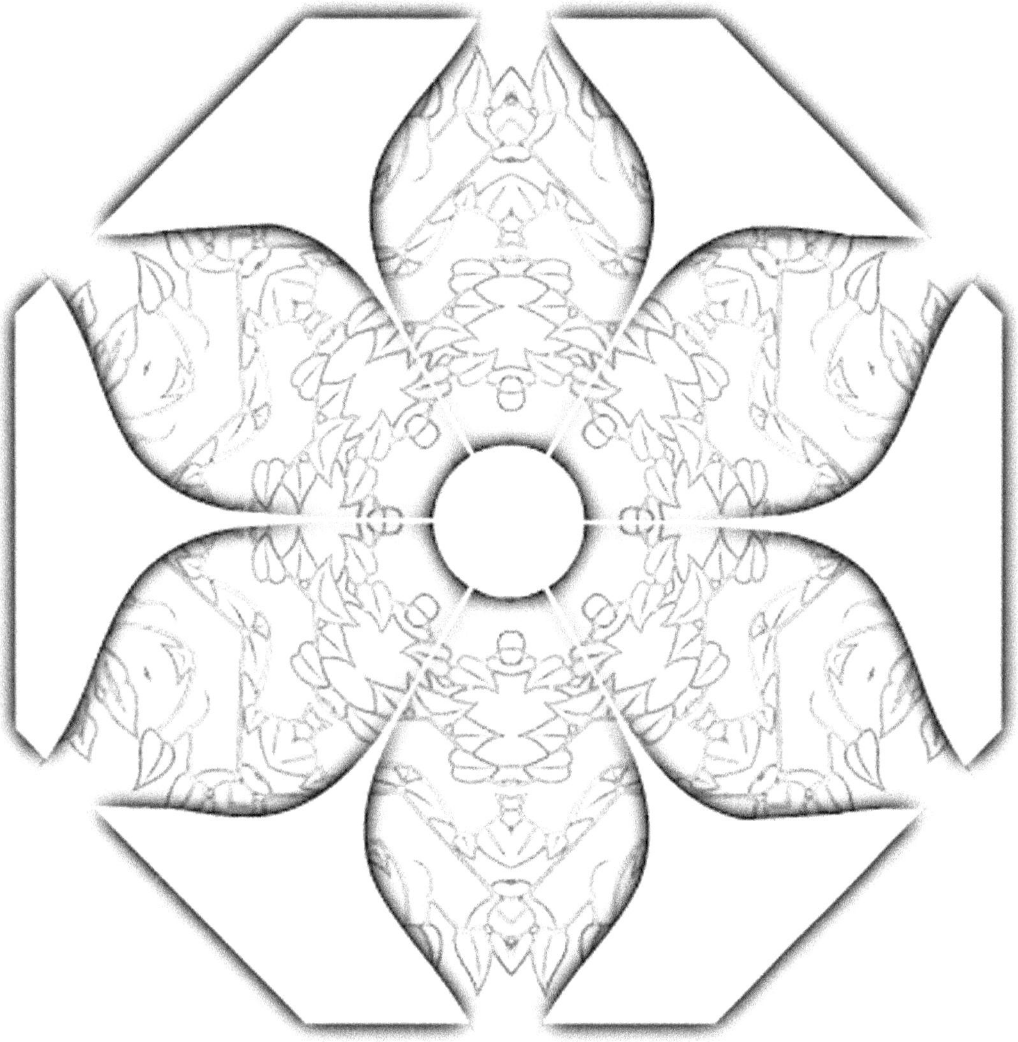

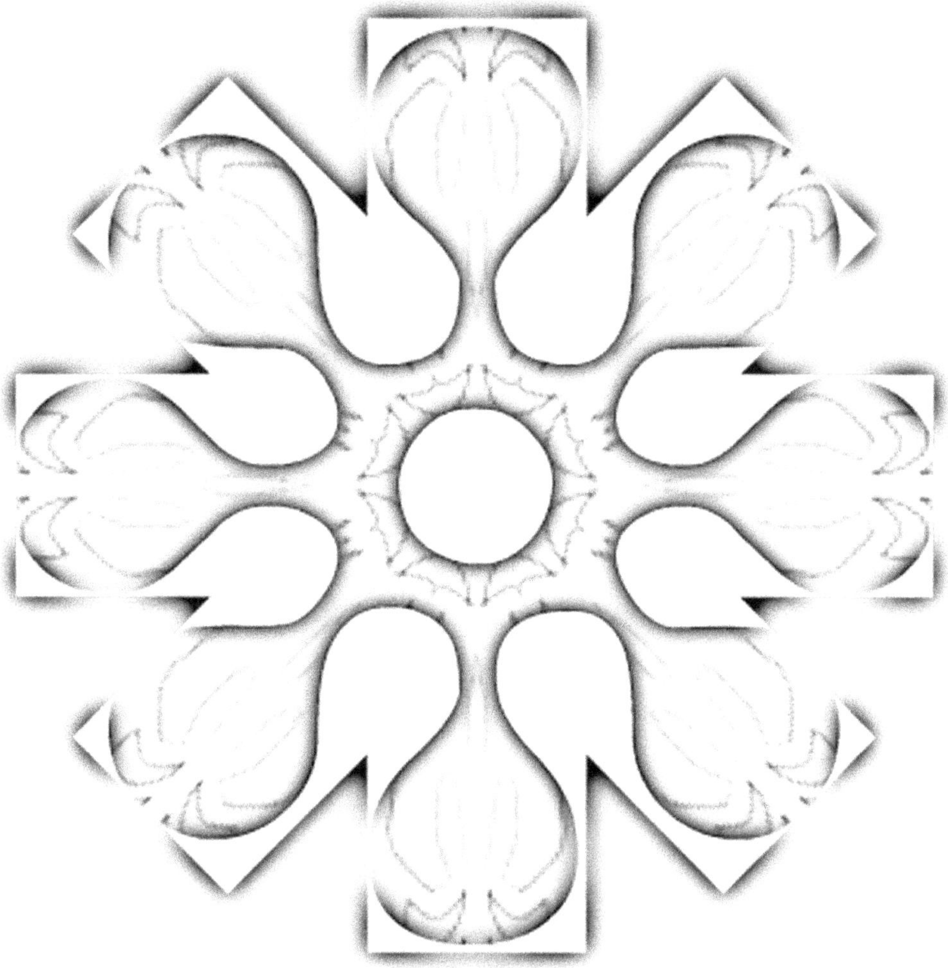

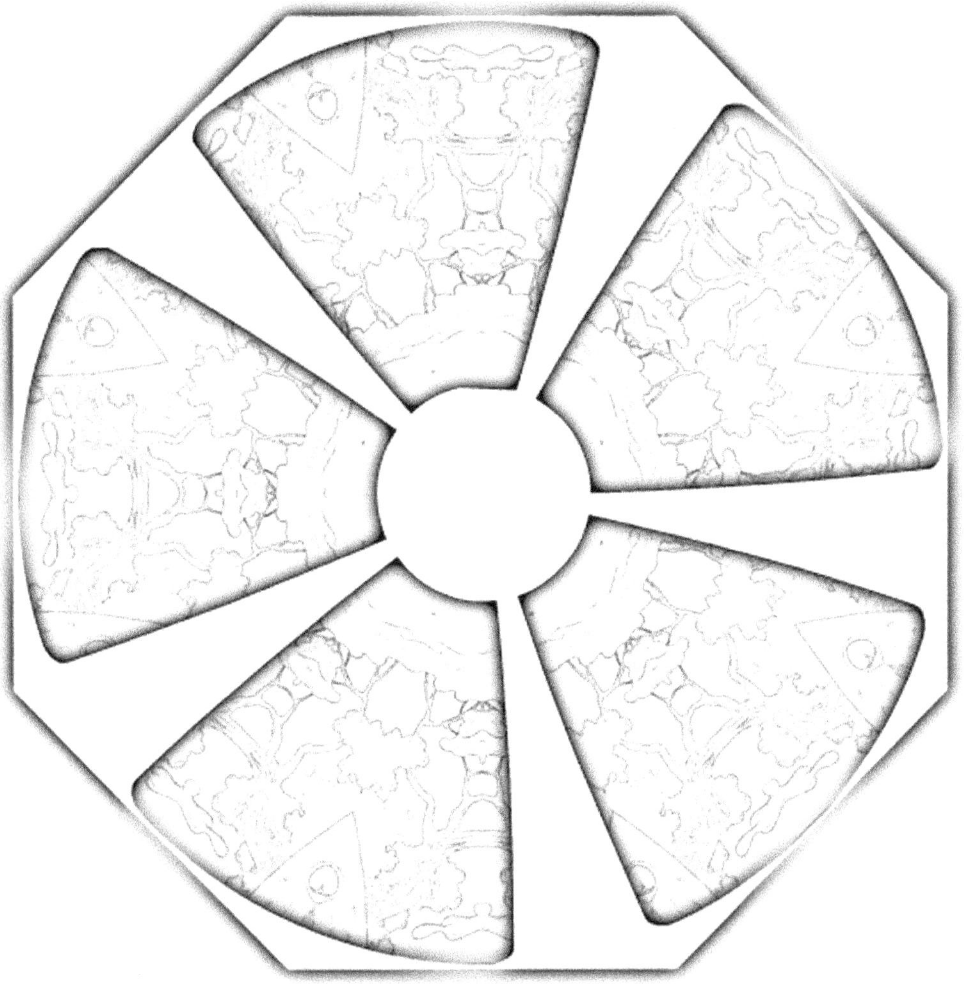

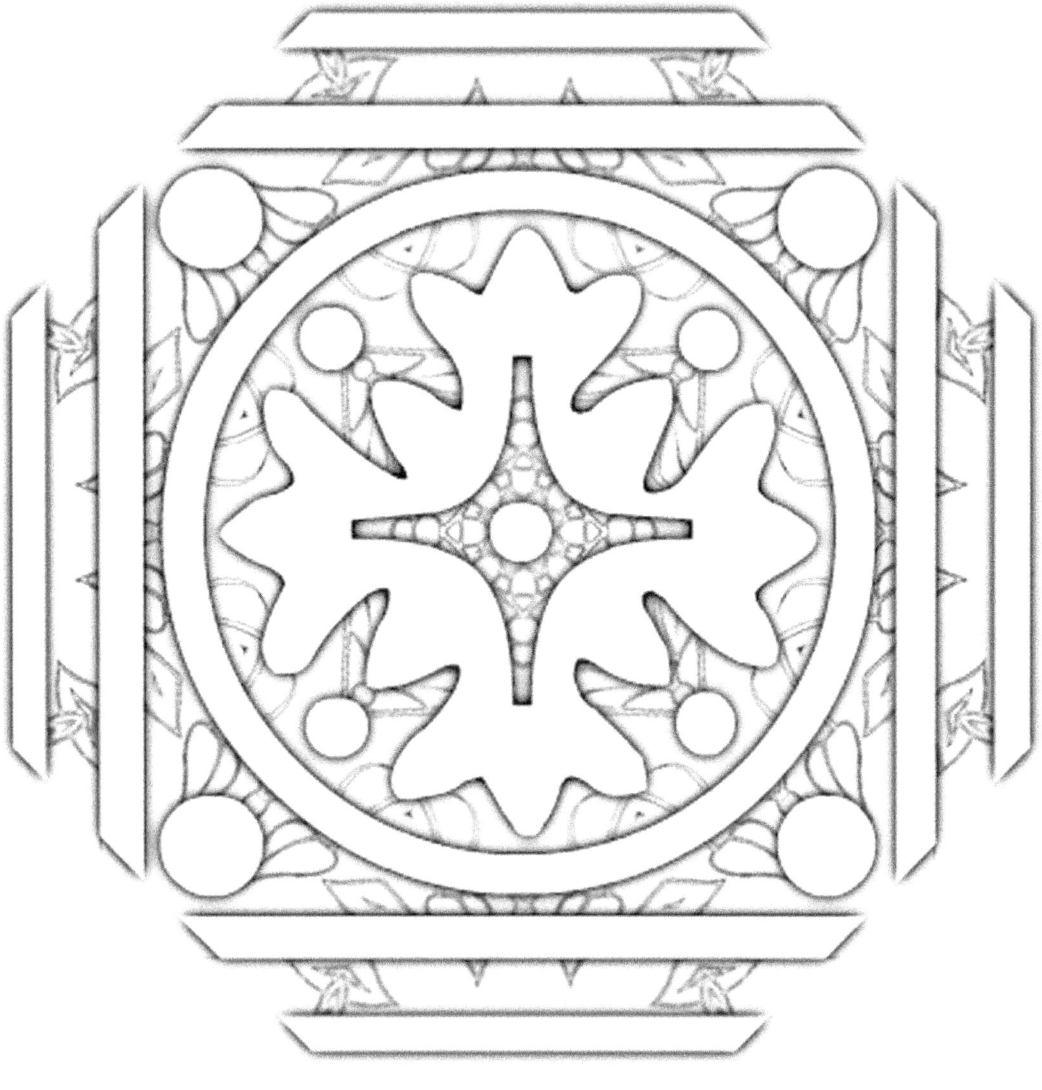

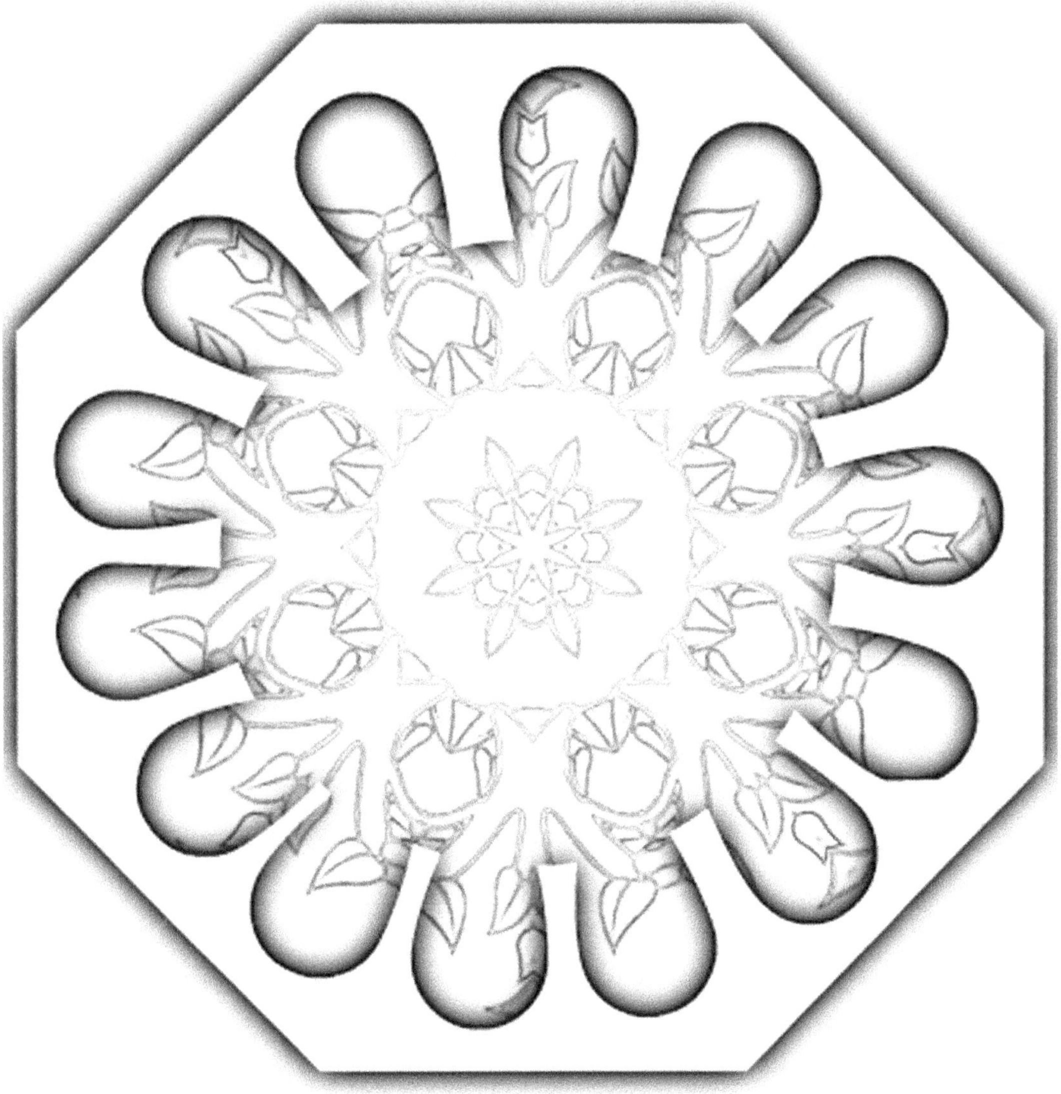

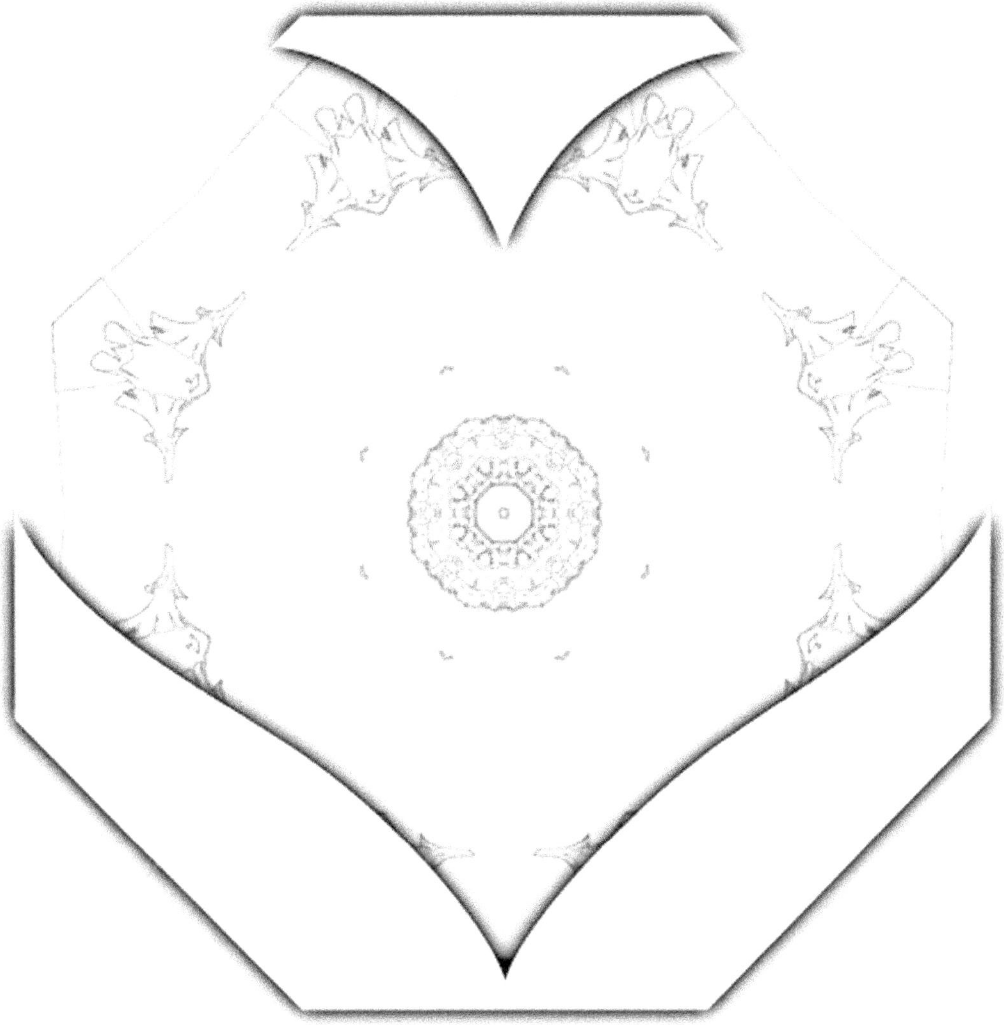

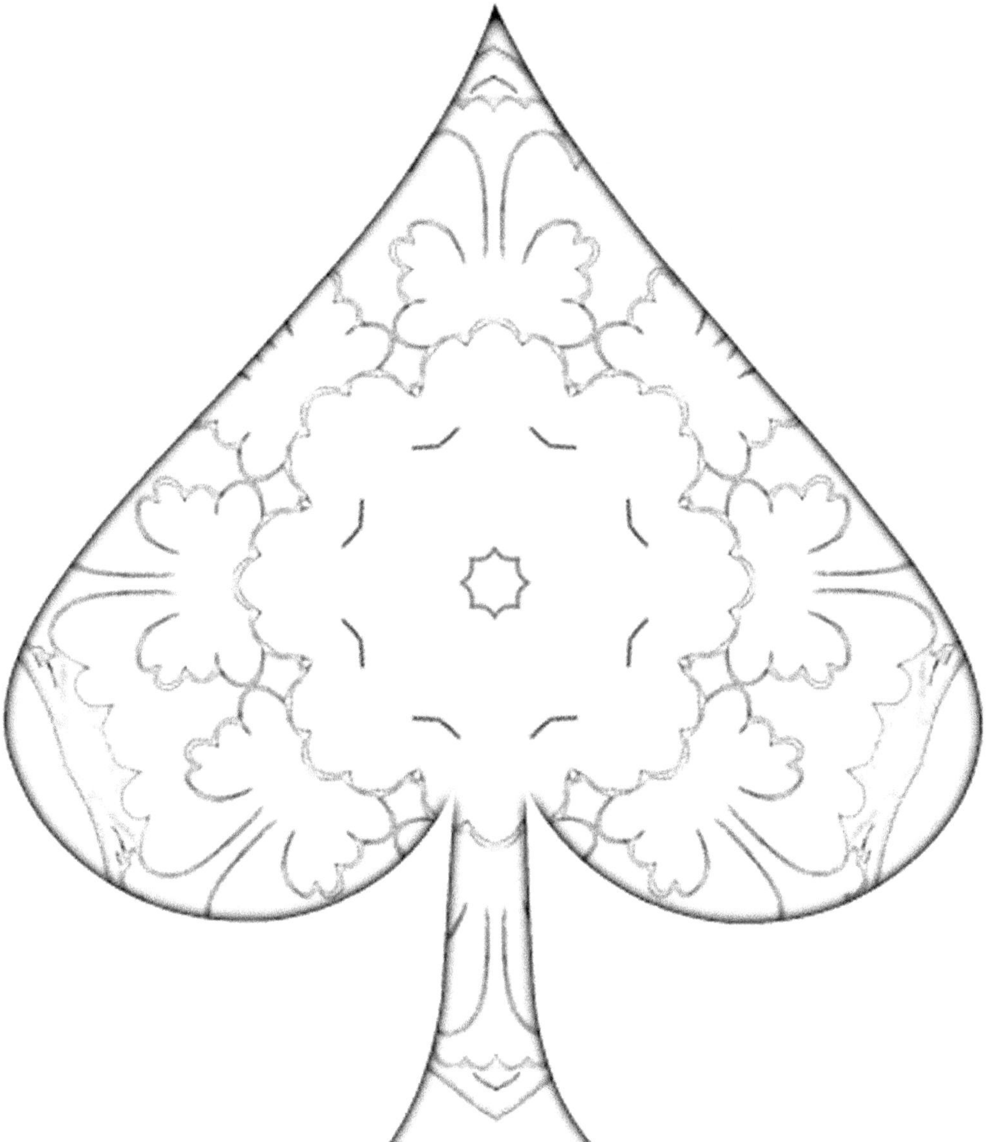

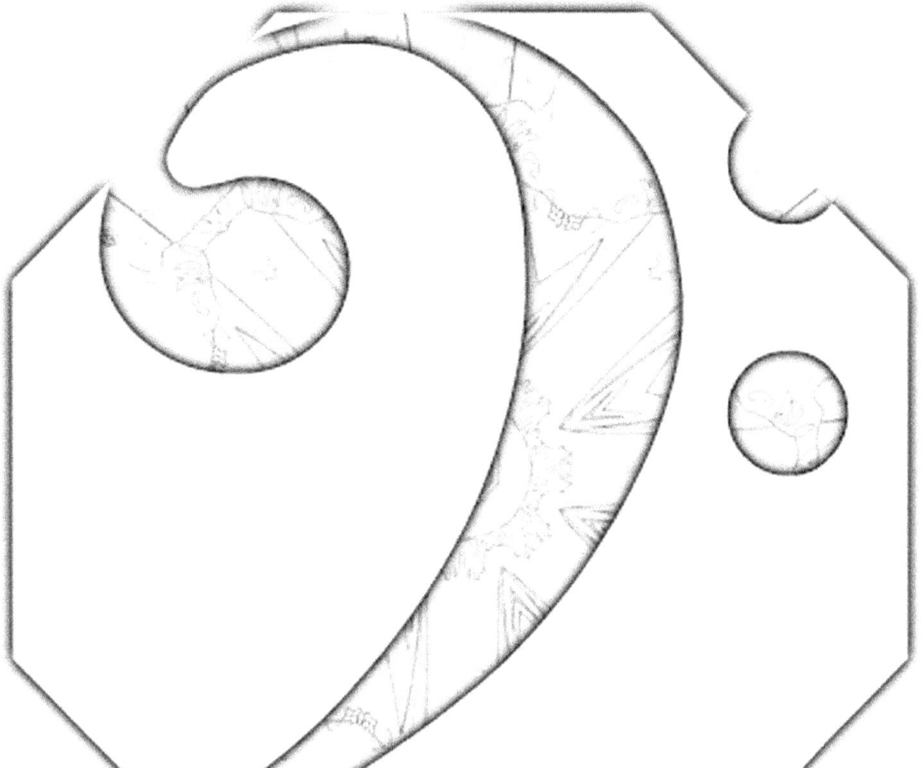

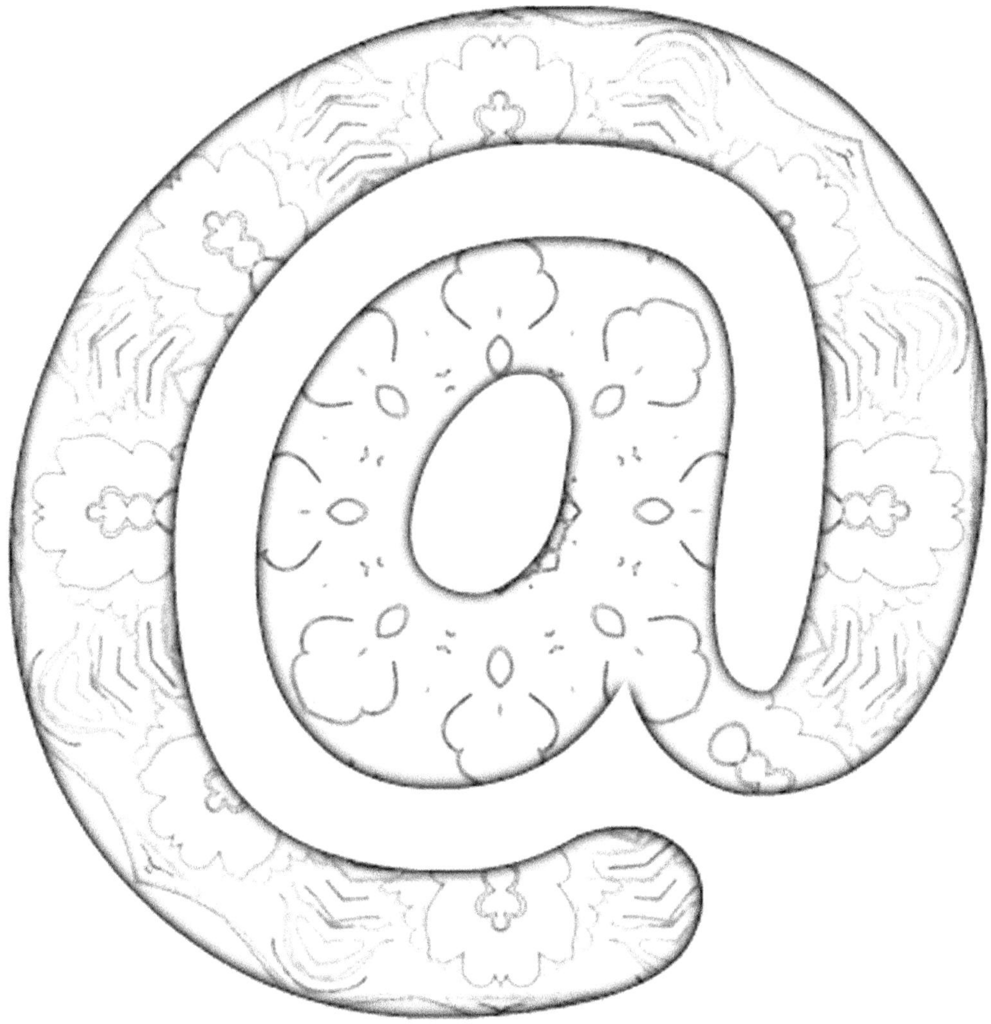

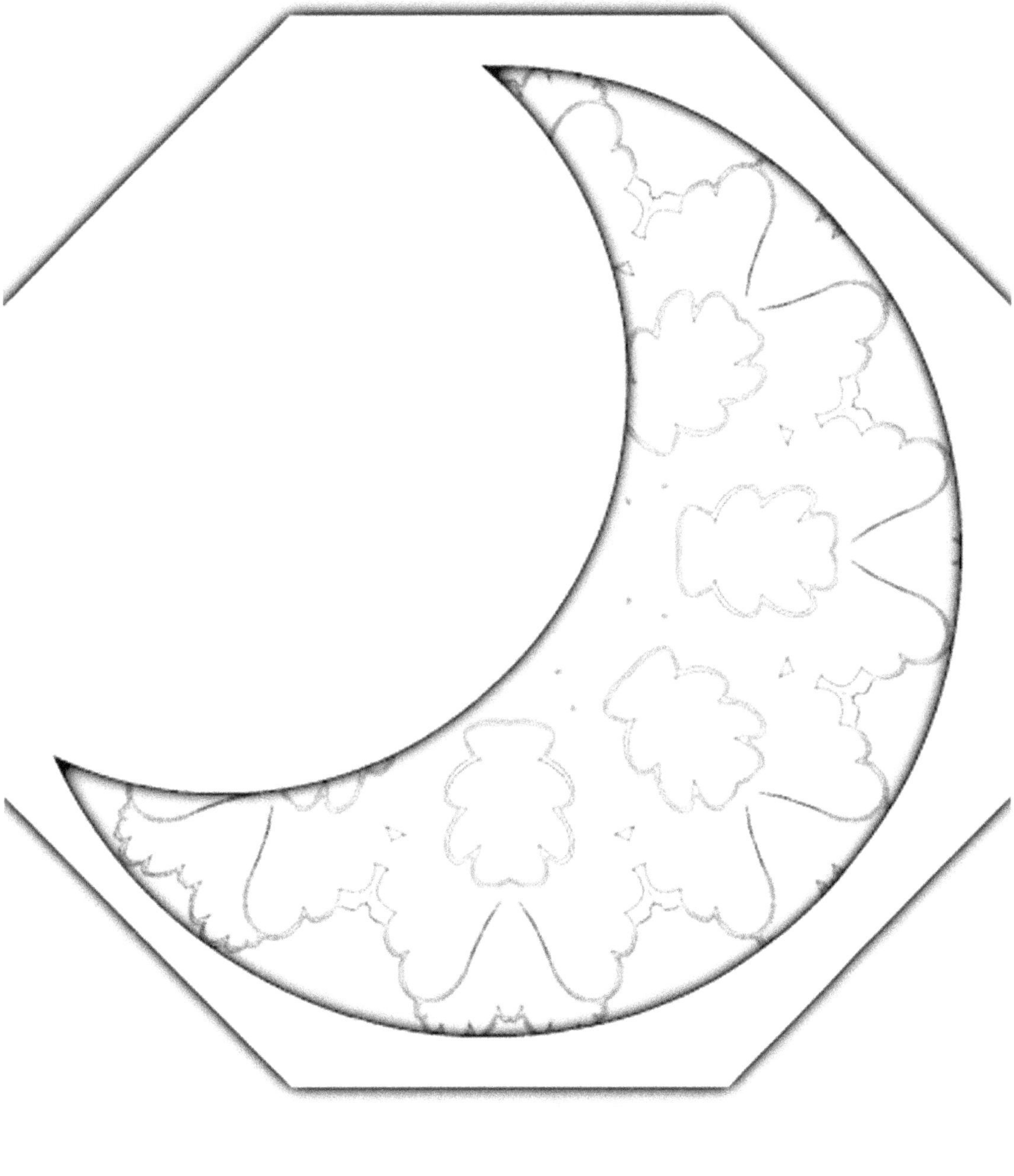

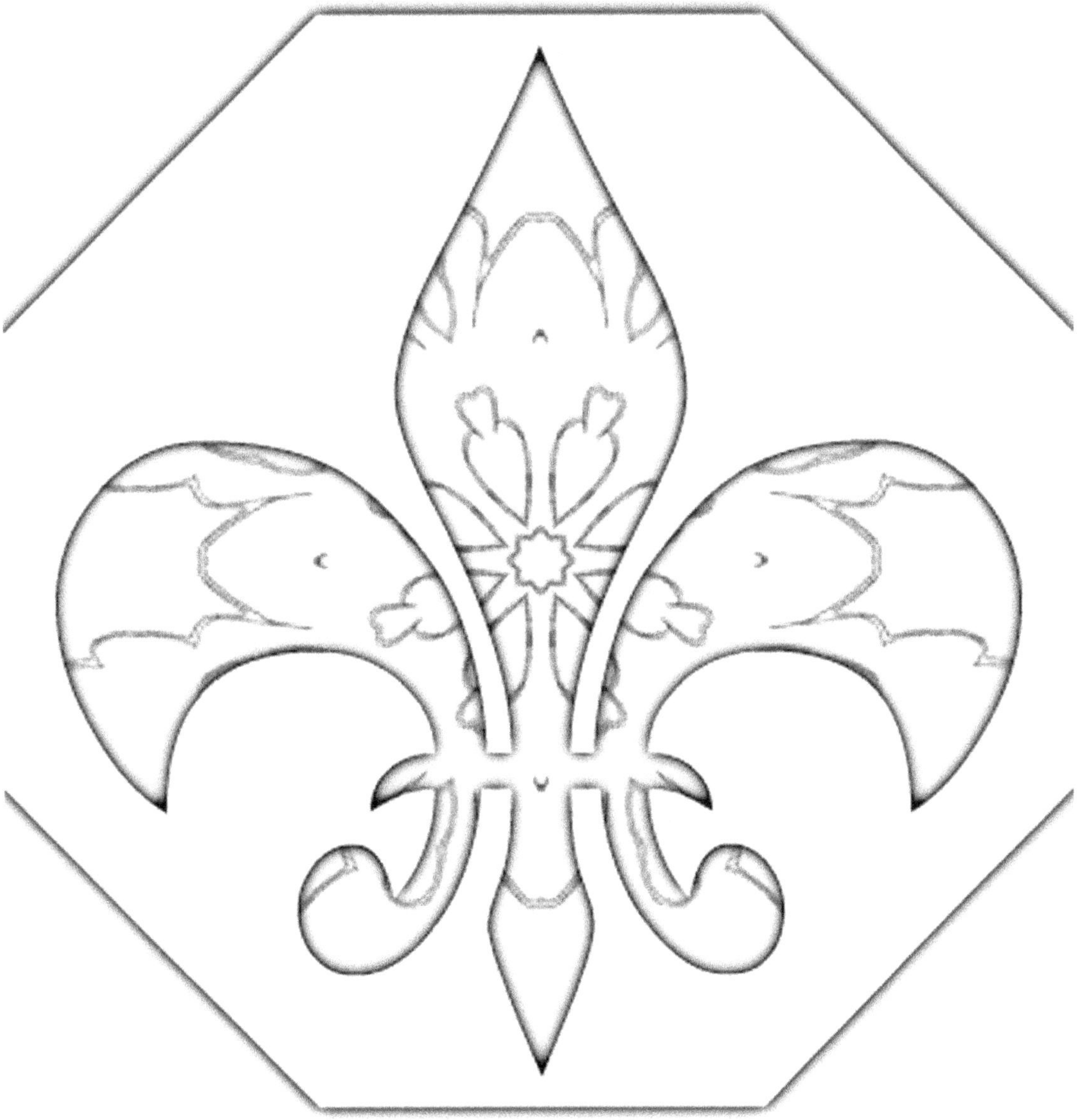

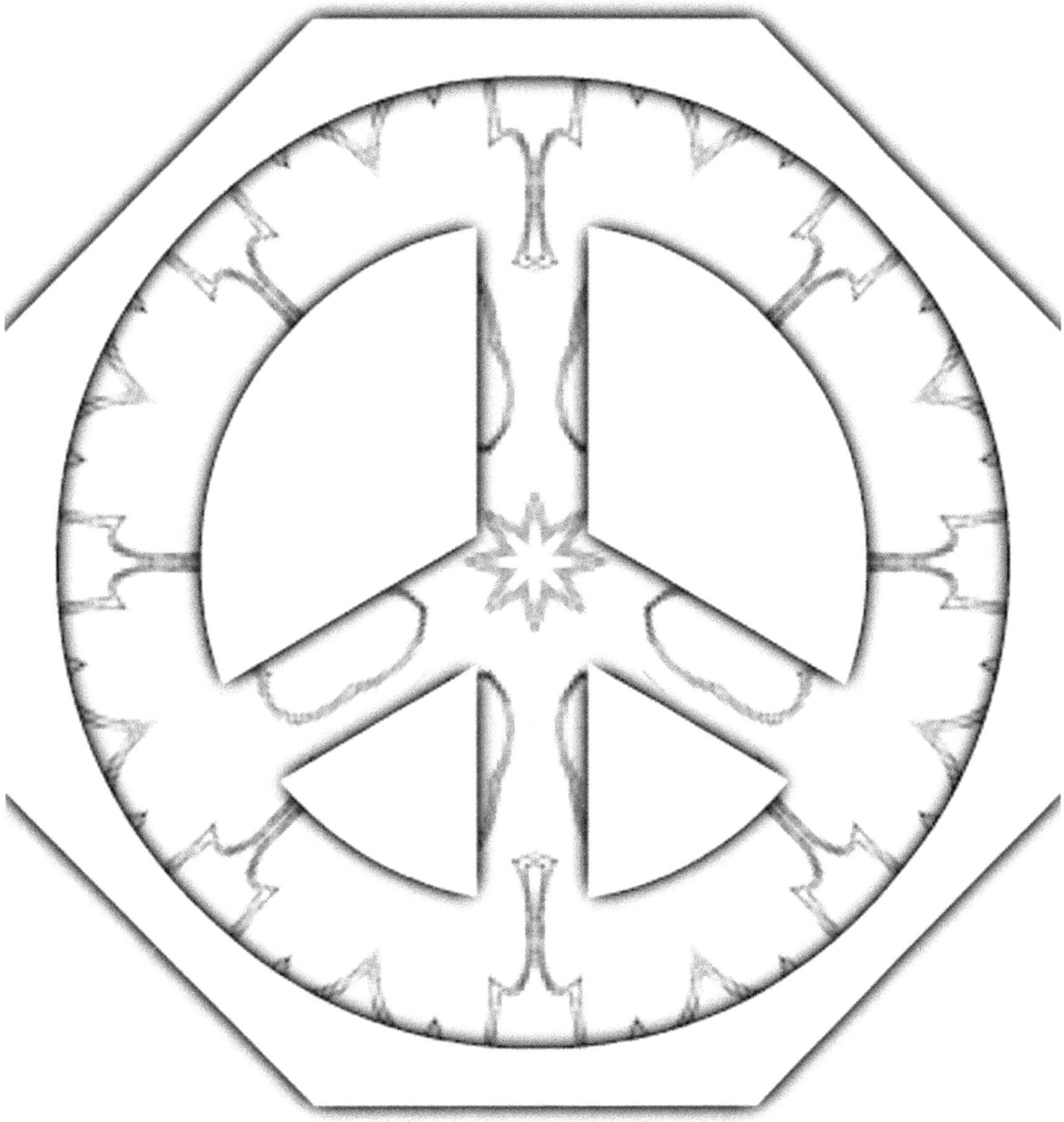

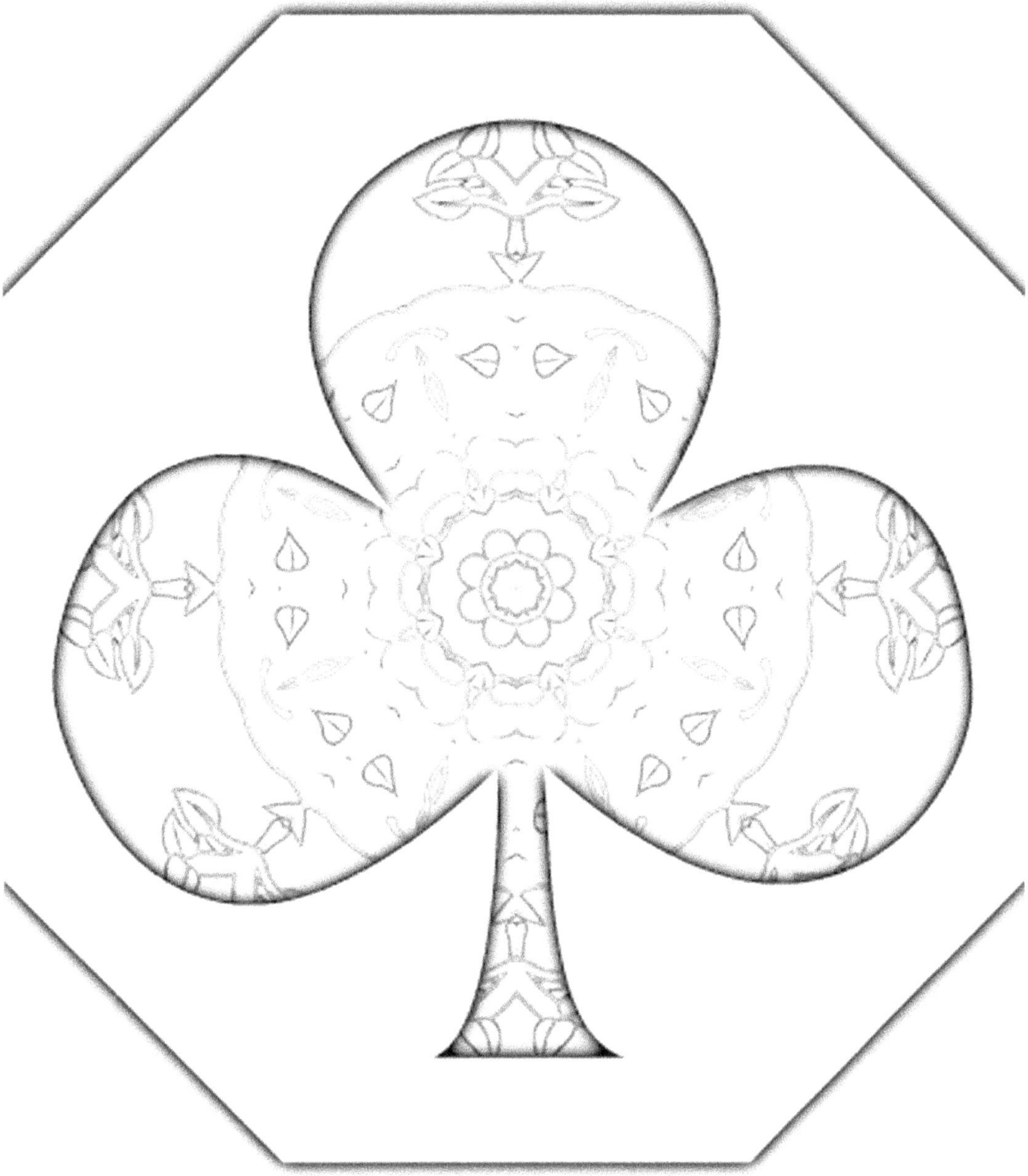

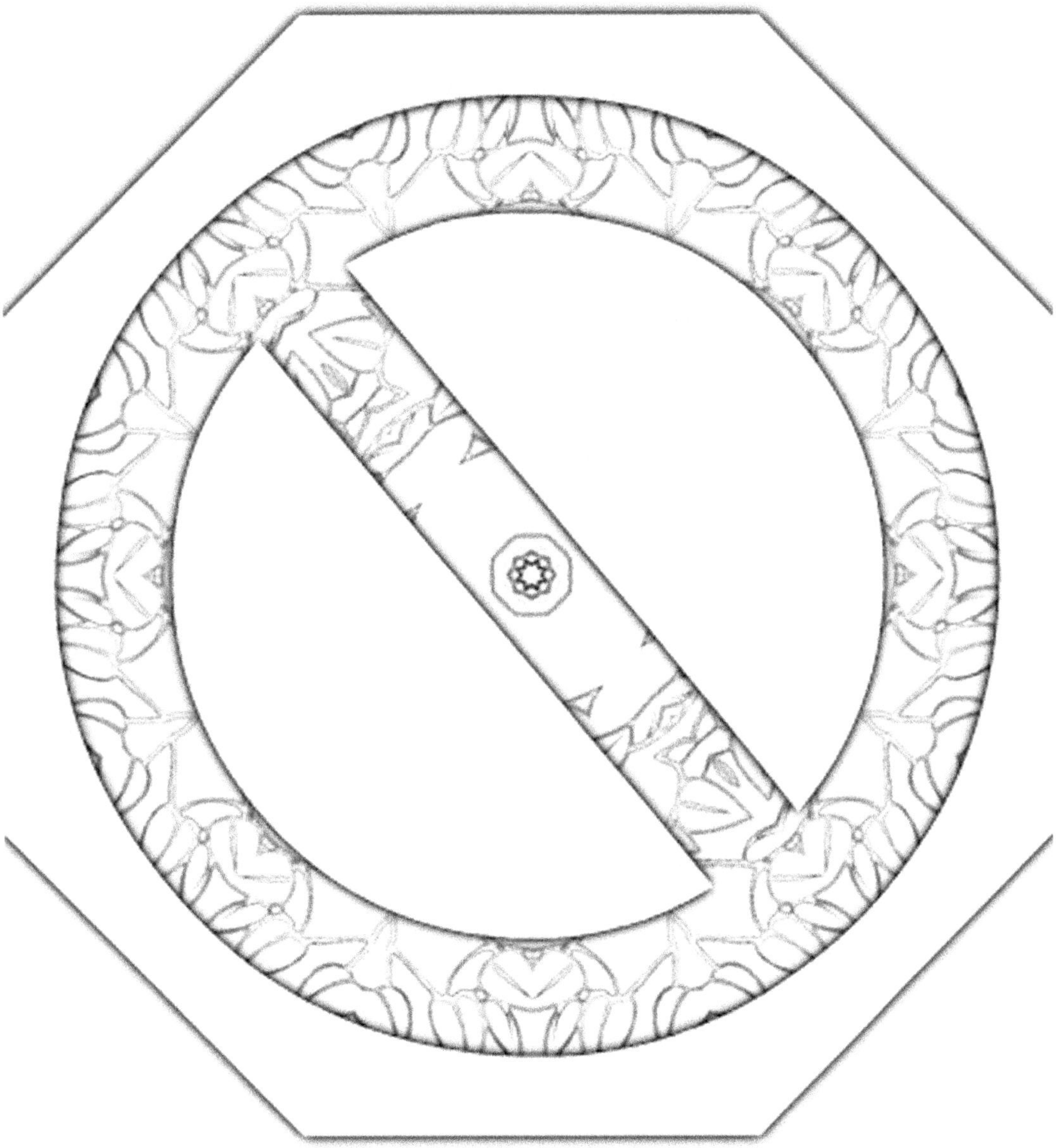

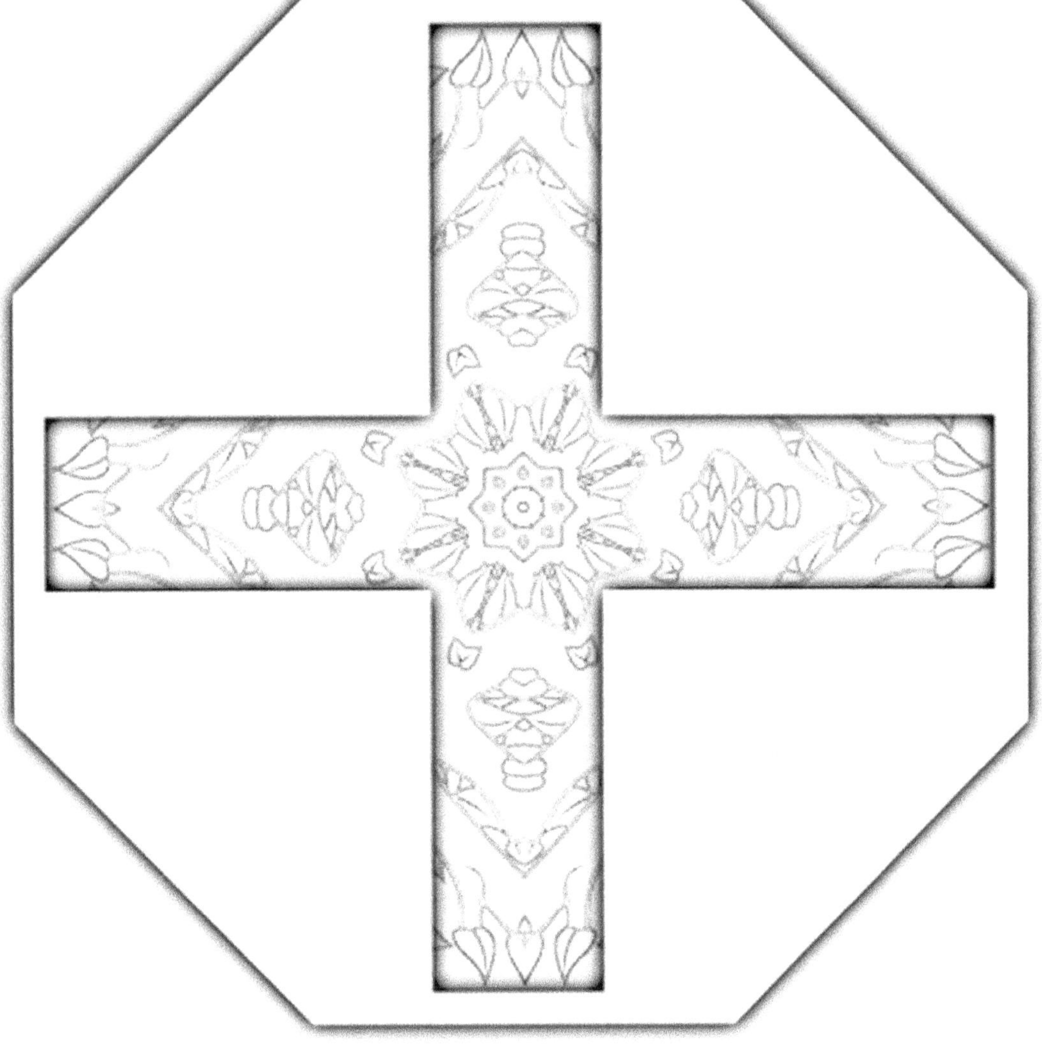

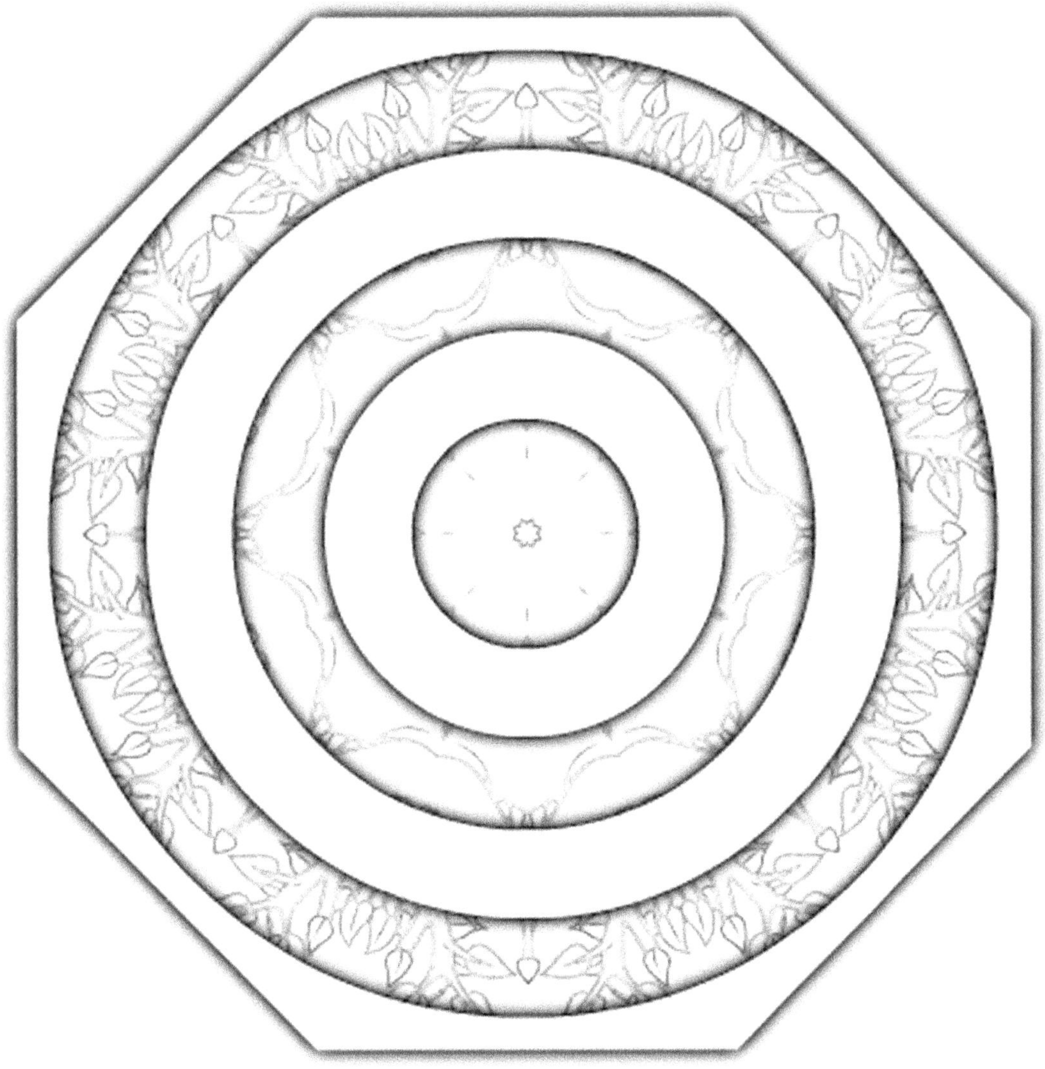

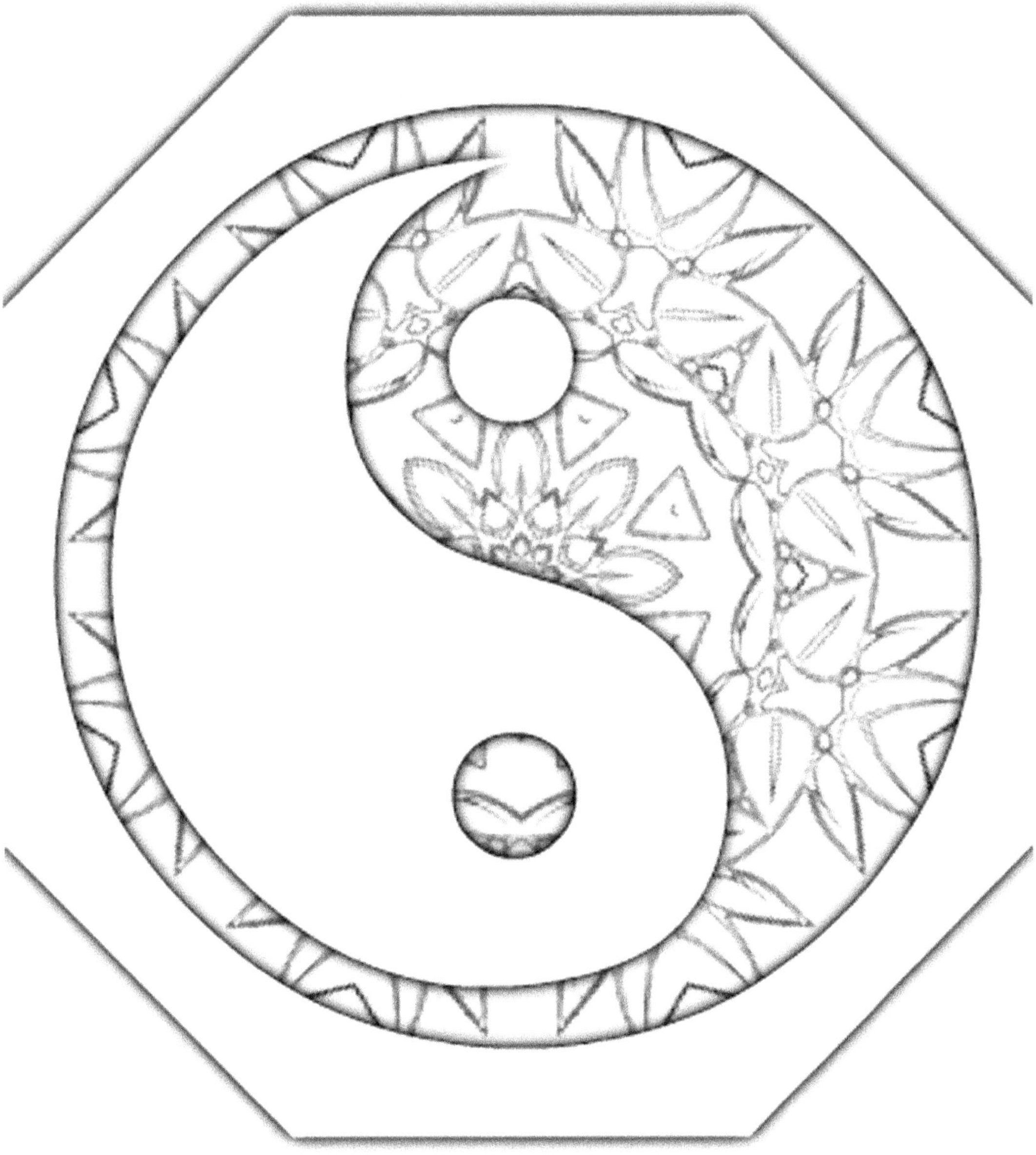

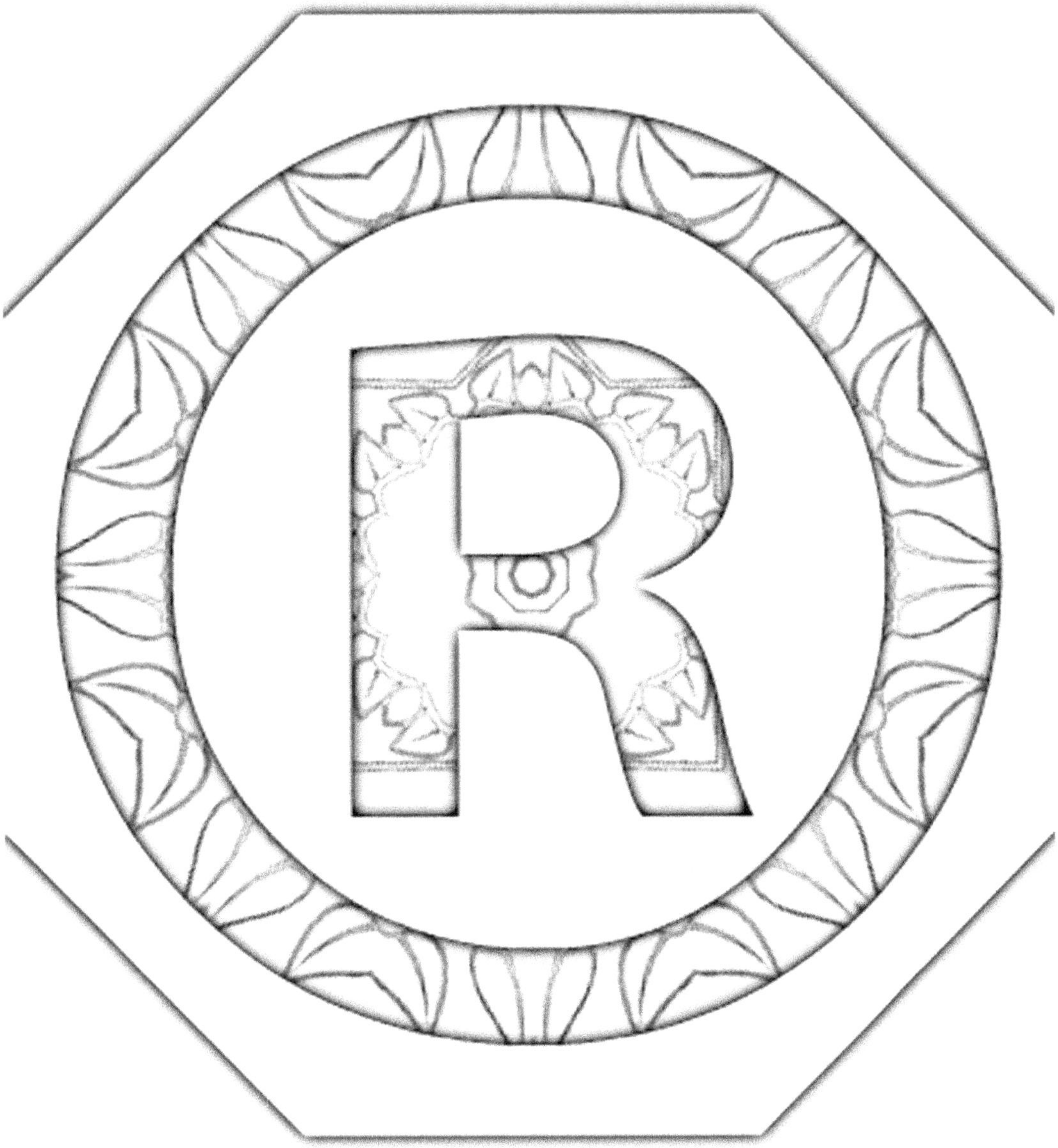
R

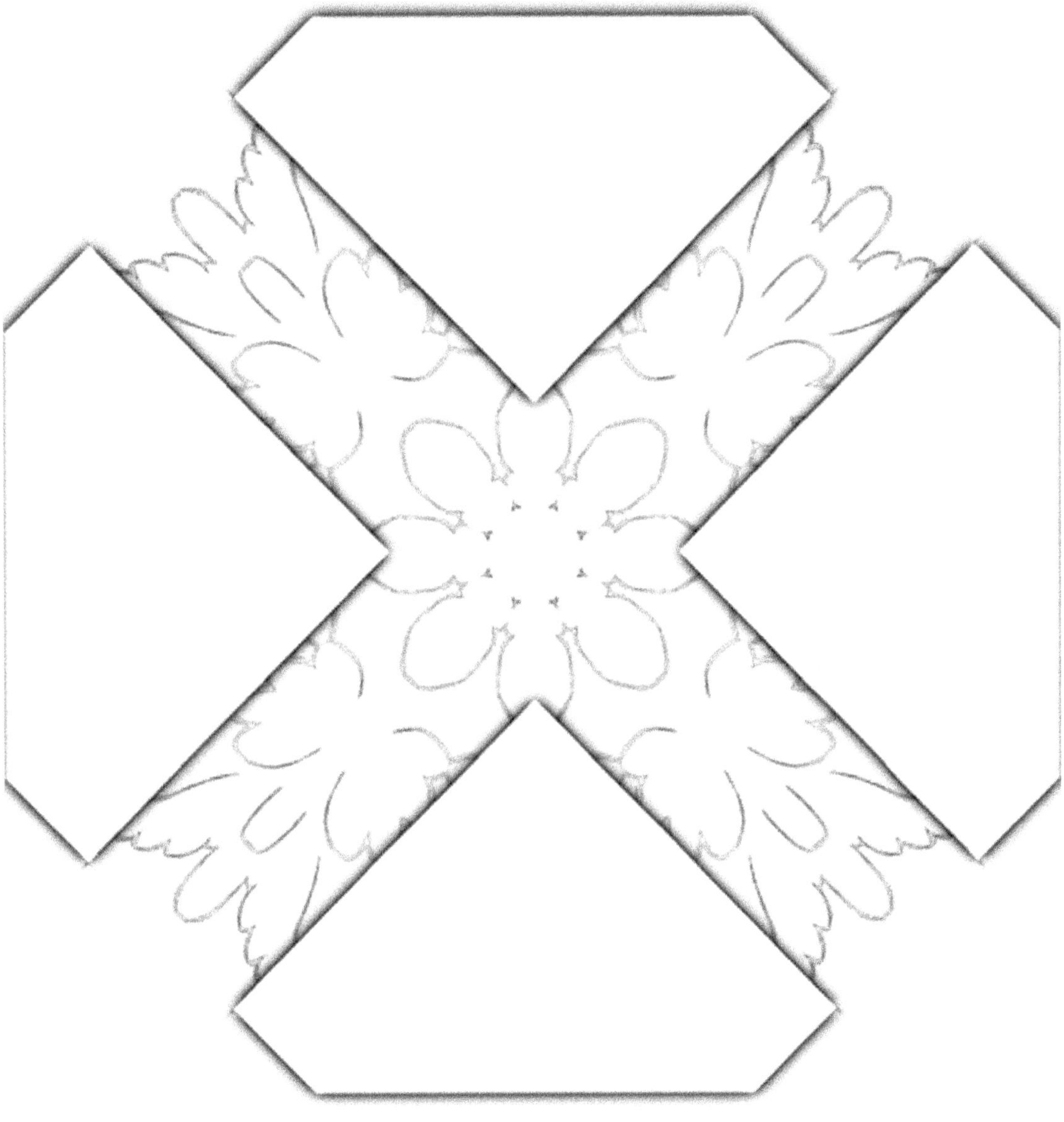

Note

www.ingramcontent.com/pod-product-compliance
Lightning Source LLC
Chambersburg PA
CBHW080646180526
45168CB00008B/3320
9781517490270